GEO

6/12
Lexile: _____

AR/BL: _____

AR Points: _____

Using Numbers
Book 1

Ann Montague-Smith

QEB Publishing, Inc.

First published in the UK in 2005 by
QEB Publishing, Inc.
23062 La Cadena Drive
Laguna Hills, CA 92653

www.qeb-publishing.com

Library of Congress Control Number: 2005921182

ISBN 1-59566-095-X

Written by Ann Montague-Smith
Designed and edited by The Complete Works
Illustrated by Peter Lawson
Photography by Steve Lumb

Publisher Steve Evans
Creative Director Louise Morley
Editorial Manager Jean Coppendale

Printed and bound in China

With thanks to:

Contents

Counting to 20

Match the numbers with the insects.

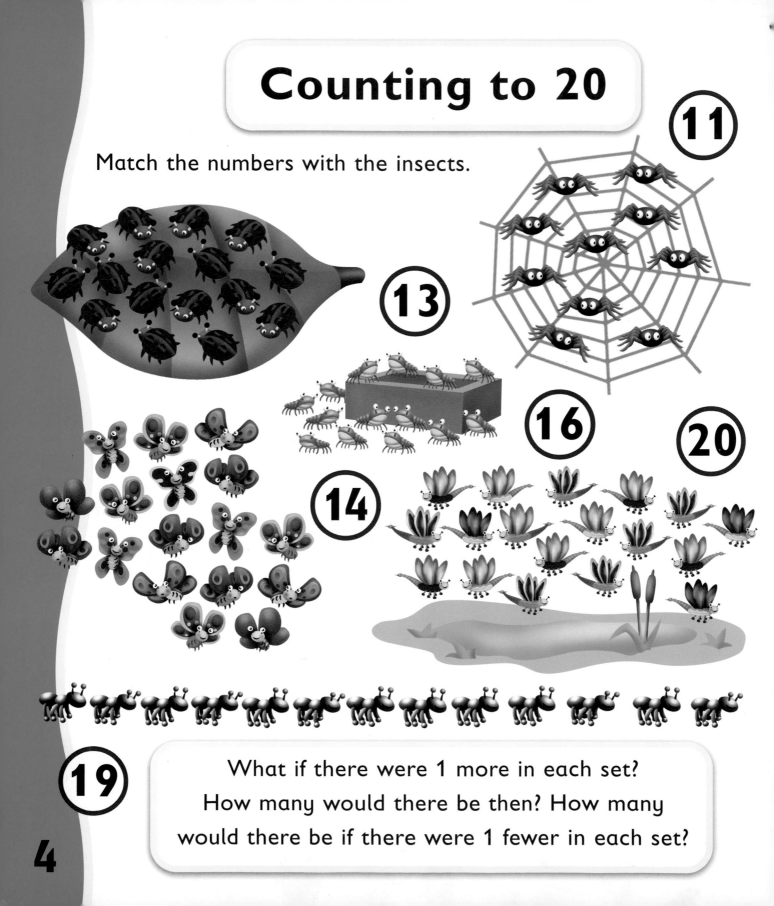

⑪

⑬

⑯

⑳

⑭

⑲

What if there were 1 more in each set?
How many would there be then? How many
would there be if there were 1 fewer in each set?

4

18

15

10

Try this

Take turns with a friend to get an armful of toys. Ask your friend to count the toys. Now you count them. Do you agree? Make piles of toys for 10, 13, 15… up to 20.

12

17

5

Estimating

Get 30 board game tokens. Take a big handful of tokens and put them onto the carpet below. Guess how many there are. Now count them to check.

Do this 5 more times.

Now try this

Use handfuls of straws instead of tokens. Estimate and count to check. Do this 5 more times.

Numbers to 30

Play this game with a friend. You will need die and a token each. Take turns to roll the die. Move your token that number of spaces. Say the number where your token lands. The winner is the first one to reach the finish.

Start

1
2
3
4
5
6
7
8
9
10
11
12
13
14
15

Play the game again. This time, start at the end and work backwards along the track.

16 17 18 19 20 21 22 23 24 25 26 27 28 29 30

Finish

9

Place value

Throw a coin onto the spinner. Take that number of tokens and put them on the Ones planet. When you have 10 tokens on the Ones planet, take these away and put one token on the Tens planet. Say each time how many tens and how many ones you have, then say the whole number. Keep going until you have 2 tokens on the Tens planet.

Tens

Do this again. This time go to 3 Tens.

spinner

1 2
4 3

Challenge

Get some playing cards.
Take out all the face cards.
Shuffle the rest of the cards.
Say any number between 10 and 40.
Now use the cards to
make the number.

36

Ones

Counting patterns

Start at 0. Count along the track by twos.
Which numbers do you say?

1 2 3 4 5 6 7 8

Start 0

What if you counted by 5s? And 10s? And 3s?
Write a list of the numbers that you say.

9 10 11 12 13 14 15 16 17 18 19 20 Finish

13

Find out

What if you counted by 2s starting at 14 and ending at 26? What numbers would you say? Now count back by 2s from 28 to 18. What numbers would you say? Now try counting up by 5s from 10. How far can you count?

14, 16, 18, 20…

Odds and evens

The gardener planted some flower bulbs in even numbers. The rabbits ate some of the bulbs. Which rows have an even numbers of flowers?

Add 1 to the number of flowers in each row. Now which rows have even numbers of flowers?

Try this

What if you add 2 flowers
to each row?
Which would be even now?
Which would be odd?
What if you added 3 flowers?

15

Making comparisons

Decide which group of animals has more in each pair of groups below. Say how many more there are.

Count each set of animals below:
Say the number that is 1 more.
Say the number that is 1 less.
Say the number that is 10 more.
Say the number that is 10 less.

Now try this

Choose a page in this book between
11 and 24. Say its page number.
Now say these numbers: 1 more,
1 less, 10 more and 10 less.
Try this again for another page.
You could write your numbers down.

15
16, 14
25, 5

Ordering numbers to 20

Look at the lines of numbers. The numbers are in order, but the bears have slopped paint onto some of the numbers. Which numbers have paint on them?

2 of the number grids on these pages could be placed together to make a longer line of numbers in order. Which grids are those? Write the numbers down in order.

Challenge

Get some playing cards. Take out all the face cards. Choose 2 cards. Put them in number order. Now say a number which would fit between your numbers.

| | | | **16** | **17** | |

| | **15** | **16** | | | |

| **15** | | | | | **20** |

19

Number problems

Get some board game tokens in two different colors. Jump your finger along the track in 2s. Put a token on each number that you touch. Do this again for jumps of 3s. Write a list of the numbers that have 2 tokens on them. What is special about these numbers?

Start

1

2

3

4

5

6

7

8

9

10

11

12

13

17
16
18
15
19
14
20
21
22
23
24
25 26 27
28
29
30

Now try this

Jump along the track in 5s. Put a token on each number that you visit. Now think about jumping along the track in 2s. Can you guess which numbers would be touched by jumps of both 2 and 5?

5, 10, 15…

2, 4, 6, 8, 10…

Finish

21

Supporting notes

Counting to 20 , pages 4–5

Count with real objects at first, then move to counting pictures.
Extend this to counting sets to 30, then beyond. Try to use lots of different contexts.

Estimating , pages 6–7

Use different objects for estimating and counting, e.g. coins, cubes,
board game tokens etc., so that the children experience estimating items of various sizes.
Try putting small things, such as marbles and buttons, into a transparent container, and
ask the children to estimate these. Use pictures in books. Give the children a few seconds
to look, then close the book and ask, "How many… do you think there were?"

Numbers to 30 , pages 8–9

Provide opportunities for reading and writing numbers up to at least 30,
such as finding page numbers in books; reading numbers on packaging;
prices etc. Encourage the children to write the numbers in the air with
their arms, so that they "feel" the shape that the numbers make.

Place value , pages 10–11

Exchange games can be played with coins, e.g. pennies and dimes.
Ask the child to take a handful of pennies and to count these out.
Then exchange 10 pennies for a dime. Then ask, "How much money
do you have?" Children can use playing cards to make two-digit numbers.
They read the number and say how many tens and how many ones.

Counting patterns, pages 12–13

Practice saying the patterns for counting by 2s from 0 to 20 and back again. Do this for 5s, 10s, and 3s up to about 30. When children are confident with this, they can say the patterns backwards, starting with 20, then 30. Children may like to sing the counting patterns to music.

Odds and evens, pages 14–15

Where children are counting objects, they can pair these to see if they are even (pairs with no odd ones) or odd (always 1 left over). Encourage children to recognize that even numbers always have 0, 2, 4, 6, or 8 in their ones place, and that odd numbers always have 1, 3, 5, 7, or 9.

Making comparisons, pages 16–17

Children can compare numbers that they find around them, such as numbers in books, on toys, etc. They can say, of two numbers, which is more/less, and what number(s) could fit between them. Encourage them to say numbers that are 1 more/less than any number up to 30, and for numbers between 10 and 20, numbers that are 10 more/less.

Ordering numbers to 20, pages 18–19

Ask questions about number order such as, "Which numbers could fit between… and…?" If children are unsure, use some number cards so that they can find the numbers they need and place these in order.

Number problems, 20–21

This number investigation encourages children to think about how some numbers come in both the counts of 2 and of 3. This is the basis of the 6 times table, of course. If children find the jumping along the track difficult, suggest that they use their fingers to keep track of each jump of 2 or 3.

Using this book

The illustrations in this book are bright, cheerful and colorful, and are designed to capture children's interest. Sit somewhere comfortable together, as you look at the book. Children of this age will usually need to have the instructional words on the pages read to them. Please read these to them, then encourage them to take part in the activity.

In this book, children are encouraged to work both practically, by counting and using tokens, and by working mentally, such as counting "in their heads." They are introduced to numbers up to 30 and are expected to be able to read and write these numbers by the end of the book. You may want to extend this to numbers up to 40, 50... if the children are confident with reading and writing numbers up to about 30. As well as counting forward, count back from larger numbers: 20, 19, 18... and 30, 29, 28... This will help the children to recognize where any of these numbers come within a counting sequence.

There are opportunities for counting by 2s, 3s, 5s and 10s. With practice at counting, children will begin to spot the patterns, so give plenty of opportunities for this. When counting by 2s, start at both 0 and 1, so that children can say the counting pattern of even numbers: 0, 2, 4, 6... and odd numbers: 1, 3, 5...

Children are introduced to the concept of place value. It is very important for children to understand that a digit's position in a number determines its worth. For example, 52 is not the same number as 25 or 520. Take opportunities to read two-digit numbers, such as 24, 13... and ask questions such as, "What number is this? How many tens are there? How many units?" Ask the children to write the number down, then to write it down again, reversing the digits, such as 23 and 32, and ask, "Are these the same number? Why not? How can you tell?"

Remember, learning about mathematics should always be a positive experience. So, enjoy together the mathematical games, activities, and challenges in this book!